Read & Resp

FOR
KS2

Skellig

Guided reading

Shared reading

Plot, character and setting

Talk about it

Get writing

Assessment

Read & Respond

FOR
KS2

Author: Jillian Powell

Development Editor: Alex Albrighton

Editor: Roanne Charles

Series Designer: Anna Oliwa

Designer: Liz Gilbert

Cover Image: © Sky in association with the Wales Creative IP Fund and Limelight a Feel Films and Taking a Line for a Walk Production

Illustrations: Karen Donnelly

Text © 2010 Jillian Powell © 2010 Scholastic Ltd

Designed using Adobe InDesign

Published by Scholastic Ltd.
Book End, Range Road,
Witney, Oxfordshire OX29 0YD
www.scholastic.co.uk

Printed by Bell & Bain
3 4 5 6 7 8 9   3 4 5 6 7 8 9

British Library Cataloguing-in-Publication Data
A catalogue record for this book is available from the
British Library.

ISBN 978-1407-11448-4

The right of Jillian Powell to be identified as the author of this work has been asserted by her in accordance with the Copyright, Designs and Patents Act 1988.
   Extracts from Primary National Strategy's Primary Framework for Literacy (2006) http://nationalstrategies.standards.dcsf.gov.uk/primary/primaryframework/ © Crown copyright. Reproduced under the terms of the Click Use Licence.

All rights reserved. This book is sold subject to the condition that it shall not, by way of trade or otherwise, be lent, hired out or otherwise circulated without the publisher's prior consent in any form of binding or cover other than that in which it is published and without a similar condition, including this condition, being imposed upon the subsequent purchaser.
   No part of this publication may be reproduced, stored in a retrieval system, or transmitted, in any form or by any means, electronic, mechanical, photocopying, recording or otherwise, other than for the purposes described in the lessons in this book, without the prior permission of the publisher. This book remains copyright, although permission is granted to copy pages where indicated for classroom distribution and use only in the school which has purchased the book, or by the teacher who has purchased the book, and in accordance with the CLA licensing agreement. Photocopying permission is given only for purchasers and not for borrowers of books from any lending service.

Acknowledgements

The publishers gratefully acknowledge permission to reproduce the following copyright material: **Hodder Children's Books** for the use of extracts from *Skellig* by David Almond © 1998, David Almond (1998, Hodder Children's Books). Every effort has been made to trace copyright holders for the works reproduced in this book, and the publishers apologise for any inadvertent omissions.

PAGE
2

READ & RESPOND: Activities based on *Skellig*

Skellig

About the book

David Almond has said of his debut novel *Skellig* that 'it seemed to come out of the blue... at times it seemed to write itself, as if it had been waiting a long time to be told.'

Such mysticism is at the heart of the novel. The story is narrated by Michael, a boy whose life is going through turmoil. His family has just moved house; his baby sister – born prematurely – is dangerously ill; his parents are anxious and preoccupied. In the midst of this, Michael makes a secret discovery in the dilapidated garage of his new home: a mysterious winged creature who seems to be part tramp, part angel. The friendship that develops between them is in the tradition of stories like *Stig of the Dump* and *E.T.* It remains Michael's secret, shared only with Mina, the neighbouring girl whose fascination with the natural world and the mystic poet, William Blake, opens Michael's eyes to a new way of seeing things. Together, they rescue and nurture the winged creature, Skellig. His recovery seems mystically bound up with that of Michael's baby sister, which finally brings relief and joy to the family.

It is a story of the transforming power of love – the kind of love that can see past ugliness and overcome fear and prejudice – and so allow us to find our 'inner angel'.

About the author

David Almond was born in Newcastle in 1951 and grew up in Kelling, a former coal-mining town. As a boy, he loved playing football in the fields above the town, camping in the garden with his best friend Tex, and spending time with his grandfather at his allotment. He also loved reading, and dreamed of his own books being on the shelves of the local library. He went on to study English and American literature at the University of East Anglia.

David did various jobs, from hotel porter to postman and labourer, before training to be a teacher. While teaching in a primary school he began having short stories published in magazines. He also wrote for adult literacy schemes and taught children with learning difficulties before his first novel, *Skellig*, was published. This was followed by more children's novels including *Kit's Wilderness*, *Heaven Eyes*, *Secret Heart* and a collection of stories based on his own childhood called *Counting Stars*.

He enjoys writing for children who as readers, he says, have 'flexible minds and can consider all kinds of possibilities'. David's first picture book, *Kate, the Cat and the Moon*, was published in 2004. He also writes radio and stage plays and adapted *Skellig* as a play in 2003. His play *Wild Girl, Wild Boy* toured the UK in 2001.

He lives with his family in Northumberland, writing in a converted attic at the top of their house. He once said, 'Writing can be difficult, but sometimes it really does feel like a kind of magic.'

Facts and figures

Skellig was first published in 1998 and has been translated into 35 languages. It was the winner of the 1998 Whitbread Children's Book of the Year and the Carnegie Medal. It was adapted into a radio and stage play in 2003, an opera in 2008 and a drama for television in 2009.

Guided reading

First reading

The first reading of the book should familiarise the children with the characters and plot and introduce key themes, such as dreams, relationships, education, faith and love.

Expectations

Look at the cover and read the blurb. Ask the children what sort of story they think this will be – mystery, science fiction, thriller...? What clues do we have about character and plot from the blurb? What is the main 'hook' in the blurb that makes the reader want to read the story? (What is this strange creature and how does it change Michael's life?) Do the children think the story is set in a real or fantasy world or a mixture of both? Ask them to cite evidence from the blurb (the reality of a garage, but the fantastical *strange beast*).

A discovery (Chapters 1–7)

Read to the end of Chapter 3. Ask the children who or what Michael has found in the garage – a tramp, an alien, a monster? Can they summarise what else is happening in Michael's life? (The family have moved house; his baby sister is ill.)

Read on to the end of Chapter 7. Pause to ask how Michael is feeling (preoccupied, worried) and why he doesn't tell anyone at school about his discovery. Is he unsure, afraid, embarrassed? Can the children guess what the creature means by '*27 and 53*'? (The numbers represent dishes on a Chinese takeaway menu.)

Friendship (Chapters 8–29)

Read to the end of Chapter 19. Why do the children think Michael decides to share his secret with Mina? (She is different from his other friends; he feels he can trust her; she has shared her secret owl place with him.)

Read on to the end of Chapter 24. What has been learned about the creature? (His name is Skellig; he has wings.) Consider what he might be – an angel perhaps. What are Michael and Mina trying to do? (Look after him, make him strong again.)

Read on to the end of Chapter 29. Discuss that Michael is upset because he feels torn between his mates at school and Mina, and he and Mina have quarrelled.

Highs and lows (Chapters 30–40)

Read to the end of Chapter 33. Ask the children to explain what has happened to change how Michael is feeling and why he excels at football. (He is elated because he and Mina have had a magical dance with Skellig when it seems they can fly, like angels.) What do the doctor and his family think is going on with him? (They think he is troubled by the baby's illness and is going through the difficult time of puberty.) Point out the cliffhanger at the end of Chapter 33 when there is a crisis with the baby.

Read on to the end of Chapter 38. How would the children describe the mood or atmosphere? (Tense, anxious.) Establish what things are uncertain at this stage: whether his sister will survive, what will happen to Skellig, what will happen to the fledgling birds. Discuss the emotional turmoil that causes Michael to black out: Skellig has vanished and at the same time he thinks his sister has died because he can't feel her heartbeat.

Continue to the end of Chapter 40. What might have happened when Michael's father says, '*It's over*'?

Turning point (Chapters 41–42)

Read on to the end of Chapter 42. What has happened? (The baby is out of danger.) Can the

Guided reading

children explain the connection between Skellig and the baby? (Michael and Mina have loved and cared for Skellig, and in return he has saved the baby's life.)

Happy endings (Chapters 43–46)

Read to the end of the story. Notice how the mood has changed and that Michael is feeling happier, more settled, contented. Why does Leakey feel that Michael has been *miles and miles away*? (He has been preoccupied and distant with worry over his sister and the unearthly goings on with Skellig.) Discuss why it is so important that the old garage is demolished: as well as it being dilapidated, knocking it down means a fresh start. Can the children summarise the 'new beginnings' that come at the end of the story? (It is spring, the baby is going to be well, Skellig has a new life, the baby owls will soon fly the nest.)

Second reading

Further readings allow children to examine the issues raised by the novel in more depth and explore the themes in more detail.

Forbidden territory (Chapters 1–5)

Re-read the first five chapters. Discuss why Michael is so intrigued by the garage. (It's forbidden territory, it's creepy and full of strange things from the past.) Ask the children what they would do if they found this strange creature? Would they tell anyone? Why do they think Michael keeps it to himself? (His parents have so much to worry about and told him not to go in the garage at all anyway; his friends would probably make fun of him.)

Emerging themes (Chapters 6–16)

In Chapter 6, pause after the paragraph about the dead pigeon. Recall other ways in which birds, flight and feathers feature in the novel: the owls, the blackbird fledglings, Skellig's wings and the feathers he leaves behind.

Read on, pausing again at the beginning of Chapter 10 to find out if anyone has heard of William Blake. Explain that he was a poet, artist and mystic (he claimed to see 'visions', including angels) who lived from 1757 to 1827.

Continue to the end of Chapter 16. Ask the children to sum up what they have now learned about the creature – for example, what he eats and why he is in pain. (Arthritis.) Why do they think Michael asks him to *think about the baby getting better*? (He is strange and unearthly; perhaps Michael hopes he has special powers.) Discuss why Michael tells Mina rather than his other friends. What is different about her compared with his schoolmates? (She doesn't go to school; instead of the rough and tumble of football, she loves things like poetry and drawing; she is fascinated by the natural world; he thinks she will understand and not make fun of him.)

Revealing character (Chapters 17–22)

Read from Chapter 17 into Chapter 20. Pause to note how the cat, Whisper, reacts to Skellig by purring and rubbing against him, suggesting that the cat recognises a kind spirit in Skellig, despite his ugly appearance and grumpy demeanour. Discuss Mina's reaction to him. Do the children find it surprising, given his grouchiness, dirtiness and smelly breath?

Read to the end of Chapter 22 and recap on what else we have learned about the creature: his name is Skellig, he has wings, he is not old. Speculate on why Skellig reveals his name now. Is he beginning to open up in response to the children's love and care?

Guided reading

Dance and flight (Chapters 23–31)

Read on to the end of Chapter 31. Focus on two recurrent themes in the story – dance and flight – and how they appear through different threads (the old lady humming 'The Lord of the Dance' and the children's magical dance/flight with Skellig; the blackbird chicks, baby owls and owls feeding Skellig, who seems part-owl as he regurgitates pellets as owls do). Discuss how and why Michael feels torn between Mina and his schoolmates at this point in the story.

Links and threads (Chapters 32–39)

Continue reading to the end of Chapter 39. Ask the children for evidence that the baby's fate seems to be tied up with Skellig somehow. (The baby is going through the crisis of an operation as Skellig has to leave.) Again, highlight the themes of dance and flight: Michael faints again – Mina says it is like his soul leaping out of his body like a kind of dance; the fledgling birds are learning to fly; Skellig seems to have 'flown'.

Renewal (Chapters 40–46)

Read to the end of the novel. Discuss how the ending suggests fresh starts and renewal through the baby's recovery, the arrival of spring, the demolition of the garage. How are the two threads of Michael's secret life with Skellig and his home life worries finally interwoven? (Skellig visits the baby and saves her.)

Focus on the three white feathers. Ask the children if they know what a white feather traditionally symbolises. (An angel passing near.) How would they describe Skellig now? Do they think he is an angel, or is that too simplistic, and, if so, why? Discuss that he is very different from our traditional image of angels. He is grouchy and repulsive in looks and habits, yet he has wings, has a powerfully kind heart and seems able to receive and give love and life.

Finally, recap on what kind of story the children think this is – does Michael go on a 'journey' of sorts and if so, what/how?

Shared reading

Extract 1

● Read Extract 1. How is Michael feeling when he steps inside the garage? (Afraid because he has heard *something* in there.) Why have his parents forbidden him from going in there? (It is in danger of collapsing.)

● Focus on the verbs in the extract, highlighting *scuttled, creaked, cracked, scratched* and *snapped*. Can the children suggest how this creates a threatening atmosphere? (Unseen things inhabit the garage and Michael is disturbing them, invading their space.)

● Ask the children to pick out adjectives that conjure up age and decay: *ancient, broken, crumbly, dead*. Notice, too, the use of repetition and alliteration for emphasis, asking the children to pick out examples of each (*scratching and scratching, creaked and cracked*).

● Circle the repeated word *something* and ask the children why this is more effective than saying *a beetle* or *a wasp*. (It is more frightening that they are not identified, and Michael doesn't know what they are.) Suggest that this will be a key feature of Skellig himself: we are not sure who or what he is.

Extract 2

● Read the extract. How can we tell that Michael is describing a dream? Can the children pick out the memories that have become muddled? (The blackbird fledglings that Mina showed him, the baby's illness, the hospital doctor who treats arthritis and Doctor Death, the family GP.)

● Encourage the children to share their dreams, then see if they notice anything else typical of a dream. (Michael tries to reach for the baby, but his arms are like stone; a noise wakes him at a critical point.) What emotions does the dream show? (He is worried for the baby, but powerless to help her.)

● Challenge the children to separate phrases that suggest comfort from those that show danger (*tucked up, soft and warm*; *squeaked and squealed, teetered*).

● How do the doctors appear in this dream? (Scary and threatening with their sharp surgical instruments.) Who *does* make the baby *good as new* in the end? Recall how Skellig seems to restore the baby to health. (He holds her tenderly and dances with her.) Suggest that the doctors and Skellig are opposites: cold, clinical, surgical techniques against tenderness, love and faith.

Extract 3

● Read Extract 3, then ask why this seems an *endless night* to Michael. How are he and his dad feeling? (They are very anxious because the baby is to have an operation on her heart and may not survive.)

● Examine how the author conveys this tension. Pick out devices such as chanting the time, emotive descriptions like *the dead hours* and *a sunken heart* and incomplete sentences. Ask the children to identify these incomplete sentences (most of the first 14 sentences lack verbs). Discuss how this makes the text read in a jolting, staccato way, reflecting Michael's anxious thoughts. Encourage volunteers to complete the sentences and discuss how this slows the pace and loses the edgy, tense tone.

● How else can we tell that Michael and his dad are uptight? (The bickering and swearing, the spoiled breakfast and smashed jam jar.)

● Discuss with the children how Michael really feels about *the bloody baby*? (He loves her and is desperately worried about her, but he also feels pushed aside because his parents are so preoccupied.)

Extract 1

Chapter 3

I finished the Coke, waited a minute, then I went down to the garage again. I didn't have time to dare myself or to stand there listening to the scratching. I switched the torch on, took a deep breath, and tiptoed straight inside.

Something little and black scuttled across the floor. The door creaked and cracked for a moment before it was still. Dust poured through the torch beam. Something scratched and scratched in a corner. I tiptoed further in and felt spider webs breaking on my brow. Everything was packed in tight – ancient furniture, kitchen units, rolled-up carpets, pipes and crates and planks. I kept ducking down under the hosepipes and ropes and kitbags that hung from the roof. More cobwebs snapped on my clothes and skin. The floor was broken and crumbly. I opened a cupboard an inch, shone the torch in and saw a million woodlice scattering away. I peered down into a great stone jar and saw the bones of some little animal that had died in there. Dead bluebottles were everywhere. There were ancient newspapers and magazines. I shone the torch on to one and saw that it came from nearly fifty years ago. I moved so carefully. I was scared every moment that the whole thing was going to collapse. There was dust clogging my throat and nose. I knew they'd be yelling for me soon and I knew I'd better get out. I leaned across a heap of tea chests and shone the torch into the space behind and that's when I saw him.

Text © 1998, David Almond; illustration © 2010, Karen Donnelly.

Extract 2

Chapter 22

I was with the baby. We were tucked up together in the blackbird's nest. Her body was covered in feathers and she was soft and warm. The blackbird was on the house roof, flapping its wings, squawking. Doctor MacNabola and Doctor Death were beneath us in the garden. They had a table filled with knives and scissors and saws. Doctor Death had a great syringe in his fist.

'Bring her down!' he yelled. 'We'll make her good as new!'

The baby squeaked and squealed in fright. She stood at the edge of the nest, flapping her wings, trying for the first time to fly. I saw the great bare patches on her skin: she didn't have enough feathers yet, her wings weren't strong enough yet. I tried to reach for her but my arms were hard and stiff as stone.

'Go on!' the doctors yelled. They laughed. 'Go on, baby! Fly!'

Doctor MacNabola lifted a shining saw.

She teetered on the brink.

Then I heard the hooting of an owl. I opened my eyes. Pale light was glowing at my window. I looked down, saw Mina in the wilderness with her hands against her face.

Hoot. Hoot hoot hoot.

Text © 1998, David Almond; illustration © 2010, Karen Donnelly.

Extract 3

Chapter 37

An endless night. In and out of dreams. In and out of sleep. Dad snoring and snuffling in the room next door. No moon in the sky. Endless darkness. The clock at my bedside was surely stuck. All it showed were the dead hours. One o'clock. Two o'clock. Three o'clock. Endless minutes between them. No hooting of owls, no calling from Skellig or Mina. Like the whole world was stuck, all of time was stuck. Then I must have slept properly at last, and I woke to daylight with stinging eyes and a sunken heart.

And then we fought, my Dad and I, while we crunched burnt toast and swigged tepid tea.

'No!' I yelled. 'I won't go to school! Why should I? Not today!'

'You'll do as you're bloody told! You'll do what's best for your mum and the baby!'

'You just want me out of the way so you don't have to think about me and don't have to worry about me and you can just think about the bloody baby!'

'Don't say bloody!'

'It is bloody! It's bloody bloody bloody! And it isn't fair!'

Dad kicked the leg of the table and the milk bottle toppled over on the table and a jar of jam crashed to the floor.

'See?' he yelled. 'See the state you get me in?'

Text © 1998, David Almond; illustration © 2010, Karen Donnelly.

Plot, character and setting

Revelations

Objective: To understand how writers use different structures to create coherence and impact.
What you need: Copies of *Skellig*, a whiteboard, copies of photocopiable page 15, scissors and glue.

What to do

● Read Chapter 10, then ask the children what Michael knows about Skellig so far – for example, he is physically weak and he enjoys Chinese takeaways.
● Examine the dialogue. Focus on the repetition of *nothing* and *nobody* keeping Skellig enigmatic. Summarise the unanswered questions about Skellig – who or what he is, where he comes from, why he is there. Then discuss what we learn about him by the end of the story (such as his name and the fact that he has wings) and what questions remain unanswered.

● Hand out photocopiable page 15 for the children to work on in pairs. They should cut and paste the statements in the order in which they are revealed in the book, so if the children think the first thing we learn about Skellig is that he can talk, they should put that first. Ask them to try it from memory first, then check by scanning through the novel.
● Ask a volunteer pair to suggest the right order and allow others to challenge them, citing evidence. Discuss how the gradual revelations about Skellig sustain our interest in him and the story, and contribute to its mystery.

Differentiation
For older/more confident learners: Challenge the children to add to the facts list on the sheet.
For younger/less confident learners: Let the children scan through the novel as they approach the task.

An extraordinary being

Objective: To make notes on and use evidence from across a text to explain events or ideas.
What you need: Copies of *Skellig*, a whiteboard, copies of photocopiable page 16 and pens.
Cross-curricular link: Science.

What to do

● Read Chapters 35 and 36. Can the children explain what Mina means when she says of Skellig: *'We can't know... We have to allow ourselves to see what there is to see, and we have to imagine'*? Summarise what we know about Skellig (his grumpy manner and tramp-like appearance, his wings, the owl pellets).
● Discuss the idea of classification, which Mina is rejecting, but which Michael's school education might favour. Briefly explain the system of classification for plants and animals established by Carolus Linnaeus in the 1700s. He grouped animals and plants by similar physical

characteristics, and gave a name to each species. This makes them easier to identify and study, but might there be some things – like Skellig – that don't fit in?
● Hand out photocopiable page 16 and review the questions. For example, the first box might be: *A winged being, part owl part human*, and for the species you could invent a name such as *Skelligus Skellig*. Ask the children to work in pairs to complete the sheet.
● Share ideas, then discuss how the idea of mysterious creatures not recognised in science is key to the story (and to William Blake's visions).

Differentiation
For older/more confident learners: Pairs of children could use the photocopiable sheet to plan an encyclopedia entry on blackbirds.
For younger/less confident learners: Encourage the children to draw an imaginary creature and label it with details of appearance, diet, and so on.

Plot, character and setting

Out of control

> **Objective:** To understand underlying themes, causes and points of view.
> **What you need:** Copies of *Skellig*, a whiteboard, paper, pens and access to computers.
> **Cross-curricular link:** ICT.

What to do
● Read Chapter 14. Ask the children to describe the plans Michael's parents have for the garden. Suggest that every house has 'chapters' of significant change. Encourage children to offer their own stories about moving or major alterations to their homes.
● Focus on the description of clearing the garden. Generate words and phrases to depict the state of the garden (*overgrown, chaotic, teeming with life*) and write them on the board. Notice the feeling that Michael is struggling to gain control, and examine techniques that achieve this (short sentences; nouns describing different creatures; vivid active verbs such as *scurried* and *squirmed*).

● Ask the children what else is chaotic about Michael's new house. (It is run down and untidy and the garage is a rubbish dump.) Suggest that the estate agent uses persuasive language to sell the potential, but a surveyor assessing the house would list, matter of factly, the problems needing repair or improvement.
● Organise small groups to scan the novel for facts about the house, garage and garden to include in a surveyor's report. Ask them to use word-processing software to set out the report.
● Discuss how the cluttered and run-down house, garage and garden reflect what is happening in Michael's life, that everything feels out of control because they don't know if his sister will survive.

> **Differentiation**
> **For older/more confident learners:** Groups could discuss other ways Michael's life feels out of control.
> **For younger/less confident learners:** Provide questions/prompts or page references to help children find material.

Dreams

> **Objective:** To read between the lines and find evidence for their interpretation.
> **What you need:** Copies of *Skellig*, Extract 2, copies of photocopiable page 17, a whiteboard and pens.
> **Cross-curricular link:** PSHE.

What to do
● Re-read Extract 2. Ask the children to cite some of the real events and people muddled up in this dream (the baby blackbirds, Doctor Death, the baby being ill). Encourage children to give examples of their own dreams where real people and events have been muddled together. Explain that many scientists think dreams are a way for our brains to 'process' the day.
● Discuss that Michael is having lots of dreams at this time because he is anxious and unsettled. Can the children recall any other dreams in the novel?

(Michael dreams about Skellig and has another dream about the baby and the blackbirds; his mother dreams that she sees Skellig dancing with the baby.)
● Hand out photocopiable page 17 and let the children work in pairs to fill them in.
● Discuss their work and elicit how the dreams reveal more about how Michael is feeling about events in his life. Touch briefly on how we also infer how he is feeling through his dialogue with other characters and the language he uses to narrate events.

> **Differentiation**
> **For older/more confident learners:** Ask the children to write a description of a real or imagined dream.
> **For younger/less confident learners:** Provide page references to dreams in the novel and ask children to focus on two emotions.

Plot, character and setting

A problem shared

> **Objective:** To develop drama techniques to explore in role a variety of situations and texts.
> **What you need:** Copies of *Skellig*, a whiteboard, paper and pens.

What to do

● Read Chapter 5. Ask the children why they think Michael holds back from telling his secret. (He feels uncertain, embarrassed, worried that Skellig might be put in danger.) Why do they think he has a burning desire to confide in someone? (He does not know what to do about Skellig.) Who *does* he tell and why? (Mina, because he feels he can trust her, the old man on the bus because that seems safe, and he also writes it down as a homework story.)

● Ask the children whom else Michael could tell and write their suggestions on the board – for example, his parents, Mrs Dando, Leakey and Coot.

● Put the children in small groups. Explain that they are going to improvise a short scene in which Michael tries telling any of the characters on the board about Skellig, thinking how they might react. Before they start, they should make notes on the characters and think about the issues and feelings involved. (For example, Michael's dad might want to call the police or social services, but Michael would try to protect Skellig.)

● Observe the groups as they practise their scenes, then invite one or two to perform their drama in front of the class. Encourage constructive feedback.

> **Differentiation**
> **For older/more confident learners:** Groups could improvise another scene with a different character.
> **For younger/less confident learners:** Discuss likely reactions by referring to descriptions of the characters involved.

Mina

> **Objective:** To understand how writers use different structures to create coherence and impact.
> **What you need:** Copies of *Skellig* and a whiteboard.

What to do

● Discuss Mina's importance to the plot. Why does Michael choose to confide in her about Skellig? (He feels he can trust her and she has shared the owls with him.) What happens as a result? (Together, they move Skellig from the garage and help to restore him back to health.)

● Think of some words to describe Mina, such as *clever, sensitive, bossy, arrogant, smug*. Ask the children to try to list good points and bad points about her – for example, that she is kind to Michael and Skellig, but can be patronising about Michael's schooling and dismissive of his friends.

● Write on the board the headings: *Description*, *Dialogue* and *Actions*.

● Organise the children into small groups and ask them first to find descriptions of Mina in the book. List their suggestions under the first heading on the board. Next, ask them to find examples of dialogue that reveal Mina's character. Again, list their suggestions on the board. Lastly, ask for actions that reveal her character. List these on the board.

● Discuss as a class, referring to the board, how the author builds and rounds Mina's character using the different devices.

> **Differentiation**
> **For older/more confident learners:** Children could plan a profile for Michael using the same headings.
> **For younger/less confident learners:** Children could expand the profile of Mina with further examples.

Plot, character and setting

Wings and things

> **Objective:** To understand underlying themes, causes and points of view.
> **What you need:** Copies of *Skellig*, copies of photocopiable page 18 and pens.
> **Cross-curricular links:** Science, art and design.

What to do

● Read Chapter 26 and identify the prominent theme: flight, wings. What other threads from the story relate to flight? (Skellig, blackbird fledglings, owls, the fossilised pigeons, Mina's clay birds and study of flight.)
● Ask the children to work in pairs to complete the photocopiable sheet, scanning the book for information.
● Discuss the children's findings. Focus on Skellig and what his wings imply. (He is like an angel, a human-type being who can fly.) How does he bring out the angel in Mina, Michael and the baby? (They 'fly' or dance with him, leaving them uplifted in spirit.)
● Discuss how the theme relates to evolution. Mina is fascinated by the fact that some dinosaurs evolved into birds, and the hint is that humans too might one day be capable of flight: our shoulder blades are the 'beginnings' of wings.
● Encourage the children to imagine the sensation of being able to fly and explain why it might be liberating and exhilarating, as it is to Michael and Mina when they fly with Skellig.

> **Differentiation**
> **For older/more confident learners:** Encourage the children to list words that describe how it would feel to fly, and to use them to write a poem.
> **For younger/less confident learners:** Support children by providing relevant page references.

Life cycles

> **Objective:** To make notes on and use evidence from across a text to explain events or ideas.
> **What you need:** Copies of *Skellig* and a whiteboard.
> **Cross-curricular link:** Science.

What to do

● Read Chapter 38. Ask the children what time of year it is when the story starts. (*Winter is ending*, narrates Michael.) Discuss why the author set the story in spring. (It symbolises renewal and rebirth.) Ask the children to think of as many things as they can in the story that represent new life, and list them on the board: the baby, the fledgling blackbirds and baby owls, Skellig coming back to life, the pomegranate.
● Now write *Old* and *Young* on the board. Ask the children to divide old and young creatures from the story – for example, Ernie was old, Michael's baby sister is young; the fossilised pigeons are old, the baby blackbirds are young. Where would they put Skellig and why? (Mina remarks that he is young and beautiful, but he could be seen as straddling both groups.)
● Suggest that another theme of the story is the cycle of life, from age and death to birth and renewal. Recap on the myth of Persephone that Mina's mother alludes to. Then compare the way age and youth are represented in *Skellig*. Although they are opposites, they share similarities: both are seen as fragile and vulnerable, whether a sick baby, or an old woman crippled with arthritis.

> **Differentiation**
> **For older/more confident learners:** Invite the children to choose a pair of young and old characters from the story and to make notes comparing their similarities and differences.
> **For younger/less confident learners:** Encourage them to read between the lines by exploring implied emotions. For example, how do they think Michael feels about Ernie living in squalor before he died?

SECTION
4

Revelations

- Put these facts about Skellig in the order Michael learns them.

He has wings.
He eats insects.
He talks in a squeaky voice.
He can fly.
He makes owl pellets.
His name is Skellig.
He likes Chinese takeaways.

An extraordinary being

● Attempt a scientific classification of Skellig.

> Kingdom: plant or animal

> Species name

> Diet

> Appearance and physical characteristics

> Behaviour (such as flight, other habits)

> Habitat

Plot, character and setting

Dreams

● What experiences inspire Michael's dream about the baby in the nest?

1. _____

2. _____

3. _____

● Summarise another dream that Michael has.

● Analyse the emotions that the dream reveals.

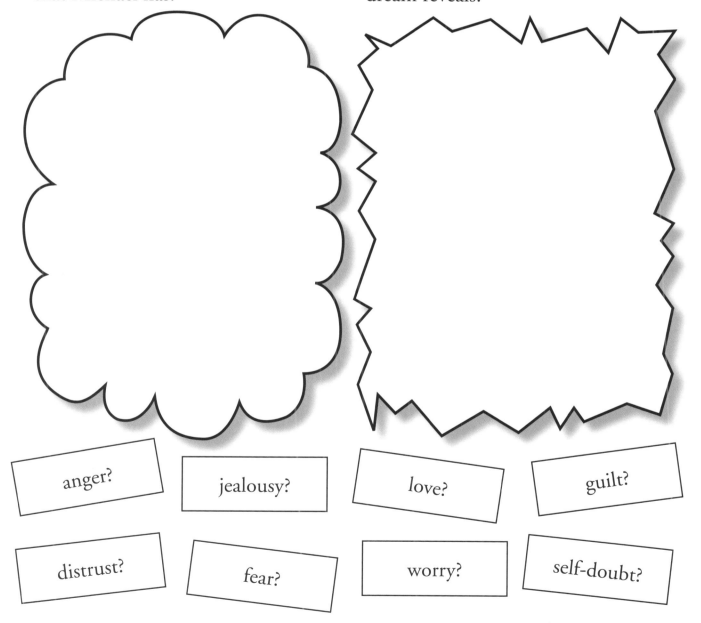

anger?   jealousy?   love?   guilt?

distrust?   fear?   worry?   self-doubt?

READ & RESPOND: Activities based on *Skellig*

Plot, character and setting

Wings and things

● Describe and explain five aspects of the story that relate to the theme of flight.

1. _____

2. _____

3. _____

4. _____

5. _____

● Describe two activities that Mina does to study flight.

Art and craft	Science

● What does Mina suggest about the evolution of humans and birds?

Talk about it

Something like an angel

> **Objective:** To use the techniques of dialogic talk to explore ideas, topics or issues.
> **What you need:** Copies of *Skellig*, a whiteboard, sets of cards from photocopiable page 22 and images/hymns/poems on angels (optional).
> **Cross-curricular links:** RE, art and design.

What to do

● Read Chapters 20 and 21. What do Michael and Mina discover about Skellig? (That he has wings.) Why do they think their questions change from *Who are you?* to *What are you?* (As they learn more about him they know he is no ordinary human.)

● Encourage the children to share their ideas of what angels look like, what they do and so on. Write their ideas on the board. Consider where we get our ideas of angels from: usually hymns, poems and paintings.

● Discuss how Skellig differs from traditional ideas of angels with his smelly breath, dirty clothes, gruff manner and apparent weakness.

● Organise the children into groups of six and give each group a set of discussion cards from photocopiable page 22. Tell the groups to use the cards as prompts in a mini-debate on whether Skellig is an angel or not. Remind the children to refer to the book, too, during their discussion. Ask them to consider whether his 'angelic' qualities change as the story develops.

● Discuss the groups' decisions, if they came to any. Divide the board into two columns and write down all the things that make Skellig different from traditional angels and all the things that make him angel-like.

> **Differentiation**
> **For older/more confident learners:** Let children source other material to support their ideas.
> **For younger/less confident learners:** Provide images and poems about angels.

Between the lines

> **Objective:** To consider examples of conflict and resolution, exploring language used.
> **What you need:** Copies of *Skellig*, a whiteboard, copies of photocopiable page 23 and pens.
> **Cross-curricular link:** PSHE.

What to do

● Read Chapter 25. How is Michael feeling about the baby – scared for her and protective of her because she is vulnerable? Which words or phrases suggest this? (*Her little hands; the gentle squeaking.*)

● Consider ways to describe Michael's feelings towards the baby throughout the story. Note good suggestions on the board – for example, *frightened, protective, jealous, resentful, guilty, angry*. Explore why he has these feelings.

● If appropriate, and with sensitivity, let children relate Michael's experiences to their own. Have there been times when they felt resentful or jealous because a sibling is taking up their parents' time? Did they feel able to reveal those emotions? Discuss how conflicting feelings can exist in us. For example, just because Michael sometimes feels resentful of the baby, doesn't mean he doesn't love her.

● Ask the children to work in pairs to complete the photocopiable sheet. Tell them to think about who Michael says these lines to (if dialogue), when and why.

● Share the children's ideas, and broaden the discussion into common feelings about siblings.

> **Differentiation**
> **For older/more confident learners:** Encourage the children to work individually and to write more detailed explanations of Michael's feelings.
> **For younger/less confident learners:** Offer 'emotions' word lists or flash cards as prompts.

Talk about it

Therapies

> **Objective:** To use the techniques of dialogic talk to explore ideas, topics or issues.
> **What you need:** Copies of *Skellig* and a whiteboard.
> **Cross-curricular link:** PSHE.

What to do

● Read Chapter 25, in which Michael is worried about the baby's heart operation. Note that he draws pictures to help him through it. Talk about art therapy, where people who have gone through traumatic experiences are encouraged to draw or paint to express how they feel.

● Identify the symptoms of worry that Michael shows during the story. He has trouble sleeping, for example, then has troubled dreams; he gets angry and swears; his skin is blotchy with a stress-related problem; his football skills suffer. Write ideas on the board.

● Then focus on what Michael does to cope: he confides in Mina, draws, writes his experiences in an essay, plays football with his mates. Again, write ideas on the board.

● Broaden the talk into ways of coping with worries. Talk about a 'worry box' where people write down concerns to discuss with others; art/craft and music therapy; exercise and sport. Consider how important it is to confide in someone as Michael does with Mina. Can the children recall anyone else he tells about Skellig and why? (He tells the old man on the bus, as he needs to tell someone who won't question him.)

> **Differentiation**
> **For older/more confident learners:** Children could try two ways of addressing a worry, such as writing and drawing it, and then see which was more helpful.
> **For younger/less confident learners:** Small groups could discuss what might help them cope best with a worry.

Divided loyalties

> **Objective:** To reflect on how working in role helps to explore complex issues.
> **What you need:** Copies of *Skellig* and a whiteboard.
> **Cross-curricular links:** PSHE, citizenship.

What to do

● Read Chapters 27 to 29. Discuss how Michael's school friends make him feel and write adjectives on the board, such as *embarrassed, ashamed, uncomfortable, humiliated*. How is Mina made to feel? Is she hurt, betrayed?

● Suggest that the boys and Mina represent two sides of Michael's character. Challenge the children to compare them. Why might Michael need a friend like Mina at the moment? (He is going through a worrying time and Mina is sensitive; he feels able to confide in her.)

● Focus on Coot's reaction to the blackbird: he pretends to shoot it. Contrast it with Mina's approach to birds: observing and drawing them.

● Organise the children into groups of four and explain that they are going to improvise a short drama. Suggest that Coot and Leakey turn up when Michael is secretly introducing Skellig to Mina. What might they say? How might they react to Skellig and how would Mina and Michael respond? Observe as the groups practise their dramas, then invite one or two of the best to perform to the class.

● Discuss the feelings involved and the dialogue used, and encourage the children to relate the scene to their own experiences of divided loyalties within family or friends.

> **Differentiation**
> **For older/more confident learners:** Freeze-frame the children's dramas and ask the children to explain how their character feels at that point.
> **For younger/less confident learners:** Organise the children into larger groups to discuss characters and dialogue before they rehearse the drama.

Talk about it

Education, education

> **Objective:** To present a spoken argument, sequencing points logically, defending views with evidence and making use of persuasive language.
> **What you need:** Copies of *Skellig*, a whiteboard, notepaper and pens.
> **Cross-curricular links:** PSHE, citizenship.

What to do

• Read Chapter 17 and note that Mina is being home-educated. Do the children like the idea of being educated like Mina, or do they think school is better? Encourage them to give reasons.
• Divide the board into two columns and write down some arguments on both sides about home schooling. Encourage the children to talk about qualifications, socialising with friends, the pros and cons of a curriculum. Ask what they would or would not miss about school.
• Arrange the class into 'for' and 'against' groups. Tell them they are going to plan a debate for and against home schooling. Each group will nominate a speaker to present a short argument.
• Briefly revise some of the key features of persuasive speaking: rhetorical questions, emotive language, emphatic words and so on.
• Give groups time to prepare, then invite the speakers to present their allocated point of view. Encourage others to say whether the arguments have convinced them and, if so, why.

> **Differentiation**
> **For older/more confident learners:** Invite older children to choose a point of view and write a letter to a newspaper outlining their opinions.
> **For younger/less confident learners:** Provide statements putting strong views which children can agree with or counter – for example, *School timetables are too rigid* or *You wouldn't have to do subjects you didn't like.*

Poetic eyes

> **Objective:** To understand underlying themes, causes and points of view.
> **What you need:** Copies of *Skellig*, a whiteboard, copies of photocopiable page 24, pens, images of drawings/prints by William Blake, copies of Blake's poems and internet access.
> **Cross-curricular links:** Art and design, ICT.

What to do

• Read Chapter 29. Ask the children who Mina is quoting at the beginning of the chapter. (William Blake.) What can we tell from the fact that Michael knows Blake was *little and ginger*? (He must have been reading up about him.)
• Briefly review what the children can recall about Blake from the novel, and from their own knowledge. Note their points on the board and discuss why he is so important to the book.
• Organise the children into small groups and hand out a copy of photocopiable page 24 to each child. Tell them to work together to scan the novel for information first, then explore poems, images (particularly *The Ghost of a Flea*) and biographies, and allow time for their own personal research. Encourage the children to focus on facts, quotes and images that they find interesting and are relevant to *Skellig*.
• Share the children's findings and ask volunteers to describe and explain their 'visionary images', which, like *The Ghost of a Flea*, should be something that could never be seen and exist only in their minds.

> **Differentiation**
> **For older/more confident learners:** Challenge children to write a short poem in the style of Blake.
> **For younger/less confident learners:** Provide prompts to help children structure their research – *Name some poems he wrote* and so on.

Talk about it

Something like an angel

● Discuss these cards in your groups.

✂ *Three things about Skellig that are **unlike** an angel*

1. His breath smells horrible!	2. He is dirty and scruffy.	3. He eats Chinese takeaway and drinks ale.

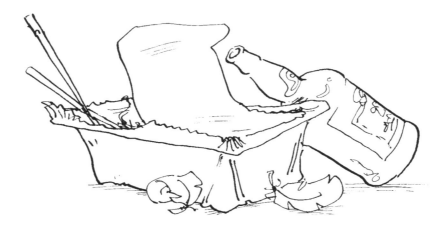

✂ *Three things that suggest he **is** an angel*

1. He has wings and can fly.	2. He has healing powers.	3. He has 'such tenderness in his eyes'.

READ & RESPOND: Activities based on *Skellig*

■SCHOLASTIC
www.scholastic.co.uk

Illustration © 2010, Karen Donnelly.

Talk about it

Between the lines

● Can you 'read between the lines' to reveal what Michael is thinking?

'Hurry up and get strong if you're going to.'

'You just want me out of the way so you don't have to think about me and don't have to worry about me.'

'Don't tell [Dad] about me. He doesn't need to worry about me.'

She came home on a Sunday. A beautiful bright warm day.

I went upstairs and slipped the baby's feather under her mattress.

Talk about it

SECTION
5

Poetic eyes

● Make some notes from your research on William Blake.

Writings	Art

Visions	Quotations from his poems

● One of Blake's drawings was called *The Ghost of a Flea*. Sketch and label an idea for another 'visionary' drawing.

Illustration © 2010, Karen Donnelly.

READ & RESPOND: Activities based on *Skellig*

Get writing

Michael's diary

> **Objective:** To use different narrative techniques to engage and entertain the reader.
> **What you need:** Copies of *Skellig*, a whiteboard, paper and pens.
> **Cross-curricular link:** PSHE.

What to do

● Read Chapter 33, then explain to the children they are going to write Michael's diary for that day. Discuss first how a diary entry will differ from the narrative: it will be shorter, more concise, a summary of events and feelings. Ask the children if any of them keeps a diary and talk about the style they use: complete sentences or note form? For example, *We did football practice...*, or just *Football practice after school*.

● Explain that they need to pick out key points before they start writing. Re-read at pace as far as *I could tell he wanted to be friends again*. Ask for key facts to note down on the board. (*Went to school. Did human biology with Rasputin. Coot and Leakey mucking about*.)

● Discuss how Michael feels about his friends' behaviour (uncomfortable) and what he might say in a diary — *C and L were mucking about embarrassing me... kept going on about Mina*.

● Give the children time to scan the text for information, then draft and edit their diary entries. Remind them to set out their text like a diary page.

● Invite volunteers to read their entries. Compare the novel and diary: both are first person; the novel is more reflective and contains reported speech and descriptive writing; the diary summarises key events and how they made Michael feel.

> **Differentiation**
> **For older/more confident learners:** Children could draft an entry for another day in Michael's life.
> **For younger/less confident learners:** Ask children to underline the key facts in the chapter.

Sounds

> **Objective:** To experiment with the visual and sound effects of language, including the use of imagery and alliteration.
> **What you need:** Copies of *Skellig*, Extract 1, a whiteboard, paper and pens.

What to do

● Read Chapter 17. Ask the children to explain what Mina wants Michael to hear. (The baby blackbirds in the nest.) What sound has he given her that she enjoys? (He mimics the call of an owl.)

● Challenge the children to think of any other sounds that are significant in the story, such as the scratching in the garage that leads to Skellig's discovery, Michael's 'double' heartbeat. List their suggestions on the board.

● Now re-read Extract 1. Ask the children to identify all the words connected with sounds.

● Ask the children to try writing a descriptive passage about another setting from the novel (the garden, the owl house, the hospital) that incorporates as many sound words as possible. Remind them that they can use adjectives (such as *creaky*) as well as verbs. Before they begin, use the extract to revise language features like alliteration (*creaked and cracked*) and imagery (*dust poured through the torch beam*).

● Give the children time to draft and edit their work, then invite volunteers to read their descriptions. Encourage constructive criticism and suggestions.

> **Differentiation**
> **For older/more confident learners:** Invite children to read their passages aloud, perhaps using instruments or other props to reinforce the sound vocabulary.
> **For younger/less confident learners:** Provide a list of sound words or let children use a thesaurus.

Get writing

Tawny owls

Objective: To write and present a text with readers and purpose in mind.
What you need: Copies of *Skellig*, a whiteboard, library and internet access, copies of photocopiable page 28, paper and pens.
Cross-curricular links: Science, ICT.

What to do
● Ask the children to think about the significance of owls in the plot of *Skellig*. Discuss how Mina shares her owl secret with Michael, which encourages him to confide in her about Skellig; also how the owls feed Skellig and help nurture him back to health.
● What facts have the children learned about owls from the story? (For example, they will attack anyone who threatens their young; they eat their prey whole and regurgitate the waste.) Try to introduce some technical language, such as *nocturnal*, *regurgitate* and *pellets*.

● Organise the children into small groups to work on photocopiable page 28. Provide access to the internet and the library and tell the children to find out more facts about tawny owls to help them fill in the fact sheet.
● When they have finished, the groups should nominate a lead writer and use the information they have gathered to draft a short non-chronological report about tawny owls for a wildlife magazine. Briefly revise the key features of report writing: formal style, generalised participants, simple present-tense verbs.
● Invite some groups to read their reports. Encourage constructive criticism and feedback.

Differentiation
For older/more confident learners: Let children use desktop publishing to create their reports on screen.
For younger/less confident learners: Provide a checklist to help the children cover key facts.

Mina's day

Objective: To reflect on how working in role helps to explore complex issues.
What you need: Copies of *Skellig*, a whiteboard, paper and pens.
Cross-curricular link: PSHE.

What to do
● Read Chapters 27 to 29. Tell the children they are going to script a short scene in which Mina tells her mum what happened and why she was upset with Michael and his friends.
● Ask the children to suggest the main events that Mina would recount, putting prompt questions as needed: *What happens?* (The boys play football; the garage almost falls down.) *How do the boys speak about Mina? What do they compare her to? How does Mina feel towards them? What does it make her feel about Michael, especially*

when he seems to defend them? Note ideas on the board.
● Next ask the children to think what Mina's mum might say to try to comfort and reassure her daughter. Encourage them to refer to the text for evidence of her character and manner and the sort of language she uses.
● Give small groups time to draft a script a scene between Mina and her mum, set in the kitchen of their house. Ask them to nominate two of the group as actors, and allow brief rehearsal time.
● Invite the actors to perform their scenes to the class. Encourage constructive feedback.

Differentiation
For older/more confident learners: Children could draft a script for another scene from the novel.
For younger/less confident learners: Provide a few lines of dialogue to get children started.

Get writing

Dream-maker

Objective: To use different narrative techniques to engage and entertain the reader.
What you need: Copies of *Skellig*, a whiteboard, copies of photocopiable page 29 and pens.
Cross-curricular link: PSHE.

What to do

● Tell the children that they are going to focus on the dreams that Michael has and try to imagine another dream that he might have.

● Ask volunteers to summarise the three dreams Michael describes in the novel and what they reflect about his feelings and worries. Briefly recap on how everyday events and people often become confused in dreams as our brains process everything that is happening around us. Invite volunteers to describe recent dreams they may have had which mix up everyday events, perhaps in a funny way.

● Hand out photocopiable page 29 and ask the children to fill it in on their own. Encourage them to think about how the dream can reflect what Michael is feeling. For example, he might be worrying about his poor performances in football, feeling a bit sad and reflective about Ernie, trying to look forward to playing with the baby in the garden.

● Share some of the children's ideas, then give them time to use the plans to draft their dream stories. Invite volunteers to read theirs out, and encourage constructive feedback.

Differentiation
For older/more confident learners: Ask the children to write a paragraph explaining how Michael felt when he woke from the dream.
For younger/less confident learners: Let the children work with writing partners to share ideas and complete the photocopiable sheet.

Goodbye, *Skellig*

Objective: To compare the usefulness of techniques such as visualisation, prediction, empathy in exploring the meaning of texts.
What you need: Copies of *Skellig*, a whiteboard, copies of photocopiable page 30 and pens.

What to do

● After reading Chapter 42, ask the children how different Skellig is from the way he was at the start of the story. (For example, he has become strong enough to use his wings and fly; he has lost much of his grumpiness.) Focus on the dialogue in this chapter and highlight the change from *nowhere* and *nothing* to *somewhere* and *something*. Discuss who has helped Skellig: the angels (meaning Michael and Mina) and the owls. What do the children think Skellig will do after Michael and Mina leave the room?

● Ask the children to think about what might happen to Skellig when he leaves the house. Explain that they need to visualise where he might go, what he might do, and if anyone might find him, as Michael did before.

● Hand out copies of photocopiable page 30 for the children to work on individually. Remind the children to use their imagination, but to try to retain the tone and characteristics of the novel.

● Discuss some of the children's ideas. Which are the most successful and relate well to *Skellig*?

Differentiation
For older/more confident learners: Challenge children to write a paragraph describing something that happens to Skellig in the future.
For younger/less confident learners: Support the children by giving them prompts and reminding them of relevant sections of the book.

Get writing

Tawny owls

● Use this page to plan an entry for a bird encyclopedia.

Latin name

Size and appearance of adult

Habitat

Diet

Behaviour and breeding habits

Illustration © 2010, Karen Donnelly.

READ & RESPOND: Activities based on *Skellig*

Get writing

Dream-maker

- Imagine and plan another dream that Michael might have.
- List three things that feature in his dream. Use the prompts to help you.

his baby sister

bird skeletons

Ernie

shoulder blades sprouting

Rasputin

wings

a football match

a Chinese takeaway

1. _____

2. _____

3. _____

Where is the dream set?

What happens?

How does Michael feel (in the dream)?

Get writing

Goodbye, Skellig

● Imagine what happens to Skellig after he leaves Crow Road.

Where does he go?

Describe where he lives, what he does, what he eats.

Does anyone find him?

What happens as a result?

Assessment

Assessment advice

In this *Read & Respond* book, children carry out a range of activities that exercise their speaking, listening, reading and writing skills. Assessment should be an on-going process, recording progress and highlighting areas that need practice.

Begin each lesson by explaining the learning objective and, where possible, link the work to other subjects. Base your assessment on paired and group work as well as individual written work.

Encourage children to assess their own work too, and that of writing partners or groups, against the objectives set, and to suggest ways of improving it.

Children can create their own assessment activities – for example, working in groups to devise multiple-choice or true-or-false quizzes about the novel. They could compile spelling tests based on topics (such as birds and flight) or parts of speech (nouns or adjectives). They could also create a picture glossary or collage (owls, fledglings, white feathers, a baby and so on) and use the images to map the plot or show links between themes.

Photocopiable page 32 invites the children to explore their understanding of key themes and language features as well as being an assessment activity.

Skellig glossary

> **Objective:** To sustain engagement with longer texts.
> **What you need:** Copies of *Skellig*, copies of photocopiable page 32 and pens.

What to do

● Ask the children if they enjoyed *Skellig* and, if so, to explain why. Discuss their favourite parts or aspects of the story. Which bits are most memorable and why? What made them want to read on?

● What do they think are the main themes of the story? (For example, friendship, love, life and death.)

● Ask the children if they have read any other novels by the author. Are there any distinctive features they can identify about his writing; perhaps a boy narrator, a central mystery or wonder, similar themes (including family illness and friendships crossing barriers)?

● Talk about Michael. How old do the children think he is? What does he enjoy doing? What are his home and school life like? What are his main interests and worries? Elicit that the first-person narrative gives us Michael's view – how he sees people, interprets events and is affected emotionally by what happens around him.

● Now focus on language features, such as repetition (*nothing, nobody, nowhere*), technical vocabulary in the ornithological and anatomical terms, and proper names or nicknames. What does the name Doctor Death suggest? (It alludes to sinister doctors whose patients die.) What other nicknames are used in the novel? (Rasputin for the biology teacher, perhaps because he has a long beard like the famous Russian 'healer' of the early 1900s.)

● Ask the children to complete a glossary of special terms which might help a younger reader or someone unfamiliar with the novel. Hand out copies of photocopiable page 32 and ask the children to work on their own to fill them in. Encourage them to use the back of the sheet to expand the glossary with some more definitions. When they have finished, bring the children together to review their answers.

Assessment

SECTION 7

Skellig glossary

● Explain the meaning of these words and phrases in *Skellig*.

Arthur Itis

---

27 and 53

Doctor Death

Pnematisation

Sweetest of nectars

Illustration © 2010, Karen Donnelly.